CHRISTIAN STUFF

What's it all about?

Derek Gerrard

Christian Stuff – What's it all about?

Published by BTC Publishing
A division of Be The Church Ltd
PO Box 403 Scarborough WA 6922
Australia

ISBN 978-0-9874141-2-0 (print)
ISBN 978-0-9874141-3-7 (eBook)

www.bethechurch.org.au

This book is dedicated to you... as like many before...
you explore what all this Christian Stuff is all about.

Contents

How to use this book

This book is simply intended to give you a quick start on understanding what this Christian Stuff is all about. There are just 6 chapters – each of which you can read in a couple of minutes – that finish with a number of questions to help you explore the topic further.

My suggestion is that ideally you don't do this on your own – but find a few other people to go through it with. Take a chapter each week and go on the journey together over six weeks.

At one point in his life Jesus said:

> *"Keep on asking, and you will receive what you ask for. Keep on seeking, and you will find. Keep on knocking, and the door will be opened to you. For everyone who asks, receives. Everyone who seeks, finds. And to everyone who knocks, the door will be opened."*

If you are reading this book, I imagine you have some desire to find out more about the Christian faith. My prayer is that, as Jesus said, "as you seek you will find". Only He really knows where you are at and what you need to hear.

Let's get started...

1. The Bible

1. The Bible

There are probably a lot of places we could begin but given so much of what we will talk about comes from the Bible – that's where we are going to start.

The Bible is the best selling book of all time. It's hard to work out exactly how many bibles have been sold, but the Bible Society estimates that over the last 150 years, 6 billion copies were printed.

It's an amazing book. It was written over a 1,500 year period from 1,400BC to 100AD. It was written by over 40 authors from all walks of life, covering 40 generations, written on three continents of Asia, Africa and Europe. It was originally written in three languages of Hebrew, Aramaic and Greek and has now been translated into over 2,500 languages.

It contains history, poetry, songs, biographies and letters with topics on creation, relationships, love, war, money, property, music, parties, weddings and even the future, as well as loads more.

The Bible is the best selling book of all time.

Credibility of ancient writings is based on how many copies of the original manuscripts are available today. It's kind of like a witness to an event – the more witnesses the more accurate an account will be.

If we take some familiar writings like Aristotle and Caesar – we only have 5 to 10 copies of manuscripts today and are convinced of the historical accuracy of their writing. Compare this to parts of the Bible where we have 24,000...

In one part of the Bible (2 Timothy 3:16) it says it has been God-breathed and has been written so that we may be equipped for life. In another part (Hebrews 4:12) it says that it is living and active. What all this means is that we need to take this book seriously – whenever you are reading the Bible take notice of what God is saying and what it means for your life.

The Bible is split into 2 parts. The Old Testament, made up of 39 books, talks about the creation of the world and the history of the nation of Israel. The New Testament, made up of 27 books, tells us about the life of Jesus and His early followers. Each one represents promises God has made and how He wants to have a relationship with us into eternity.

So how do you start reading the Bible and understanding what it's all about?

Each time you read the Bible it is good to begin by asking God to speak to you as you read. Think about things like who the author was, what the world was like at the time they wrote and what the message was they were trying to give. Finally, make sure you think about how you can apply what you have read to your life – that's a good thing to ask God about.

The Bible isn't really a book that you read from the front cover to the back cover. You could start at the beginning with the book of Genesis but a good place to start is by reading through the verses that we reference in this book.

Another good place to start is with one of the books that talks about Jesus' life: Matthew, Mark, Luke or John and follow that up with the book called Acts – it talks about the life of His early followers.

Questions

- What is your favourite book and why is it your favourite?

- Have you read any of the Bible before? What do you think of it?

- Why do you think the Bible is the best selling book of all time?

- What do you think the purpose of the Bible is?

- Do you think you will read some of the Bible now?

2. Creation

2. Creation

Let's go right back to the beginning – the place where God created the heavens and the earth.

Genesis 1:1 says in the beginning God created. It's like a painter who gives clues to their personality and character – creation is God's canvas.

Have you ever stopped to look at the world around you – from the biggest thing to the smallest thing – where everything holds together in perfect balance - it's an amazing place.

When Paul wrote to the Roman church (Romans 1:20) he said that, "since the creation of the world, God's invisible qualities have been clearly seen from what has been made, so that people are without excuse". In other words if we take the time to look around, there is no excuse for denying God as the creator.

Let's start with the expanse of the universe. We live on a planet that is over 12,000 kilometres in diameter. 385,000 kilometres away is the

The beginning... the place where God created.

moon and another 150 million kilometres away is the sun. The sun is one of only 400 billion stars in our galaxy and there is somewhere between 50 and 200 billion galaxies in the universe. Well at least that's what we know about – it is a massive place.

There is some poetry (Psalm 19:1-2) in the Bible that says:
> *"The heavens proclaim the glory of God.*
> *The skies display his craftsmanship.*
> *Day after day they continue to speak,*
> *night after night they make him known."*

At the smallest end we look at the space between atoms, which is measured in nanometres. A nanometre is one billionth of a metre – which is about the same perspective as a marble to the size of the earth. That's small and God has created everything from the biggest to the smallest.

But its not just about size – its about creativity. There are 1.8 million living animal species that we know about and even up to 10 million that are still to be discovered. Just think about some of them and how much creativity God has shown in their design.

Even within the human race there is so much detail. Each human has a unique finger and tongue print, 100,000 kilometres of blood vessels, and an average of 100,000 strands of hair. We produce about 1 litre of saliva every day and have a heart that just keeps beating so that by the time you are 70 it will have beat 2.5 billion times.

God's involvement in creation isn't about winding it up and setting it in motion. He is alive today and is continuing to sustain and renew His creation. Even though it is so complex He has an amazing desire to have a relationship with you.

Some more poetry in the Bible (Psalm 8:3-4) says:
> *"When I look at the night sky and see the work of your hands, the moon and the stars you set in place, what are mere mortals that you should think about them, human beings that you should care for them?"*

See, science does a good job of answering some of the "how" questions – how did we get here, how do things work - but it is not so good at answering the "why" questions – why are we here, why does that work like that, why did God create the world and why would He want to know about me?

Questions

- What are some of the things in nature that amaze you?

- How do you think they were created?

- Where do you think time began and where will time end?

- Do you think that humans are different to other living things on Earth? Why or why not?

- Why do you think God wants a relationship with people?

- Do you think He wants a relationship with you?

3. Separation

3. Separation

Do you ever feel like there is something in life you are searching for?

Do you ever have thoughts like "there must be more to life than this"?

Have you ever experienced an emptiness or longing that you can't quite put your finger on?

When humans were created, everything that God had made was good and He intended that we have a close relationship with Him. It even says in Genesis that with the first humans, God used to walk with them in the garden. This was how it was meant to be. For us to have meaning and purpose in life we are meant to have a relationship with our creator.

A problem came when those first humans disobeyed God. They were deceived into thinking that there was knowledge available to them, which God didn't want them to have. They thought that by eating fruit from a tree God had told them not to eat from, they would get

To have happiness in life... we are meant to have a relationship with our creator.

access to that knowledge (Genesis 3). It's strange to think that even today humanity is still obsessed with learning and seeking knowledge, as we live in a world where information is power and we want access to it faster and easier than ever before.

As these people disobeyed God it caused separation – separation from their creator and separation from His ultimate purpose. Humanity was left feeling distant, ashamed and insecure – some of the feelings that a lot of us still have today.

The worst thing is that the separation was permanent – meaning eternal death. That might sound a bit full-on but have you ever stopped to think about what happens when your physical body dies?

There is a word called sin that we use to describe separation from God – separation that is still here today. We sin every time we fall short of the perfection God intended for us and continue the separation that began with our ancestors.

Sin has been ruling our world for a long time and even with the greatest intention, we all sin everyday. In fact, one of the writers in the Bible says that "all have sinned and fallen short of the glory of

God" (Romans 3:23) and goes on to say that "the wages of sin are death" (Romans 6:23).

If the story ended there it would be one of the unhappiest endings you have ever heard - but it's not because our God, our creator, loves us so much. He realised that the only way to save us from separation was to face the sin of all humanity Himself. He did this with the ultimate sacrifice – giving over His Son, who lived a life without sin and paid the price in our place.

What God's Son did and endured on our behalf was amazing. If the price of sin is eternal death then he overcame death to give us a passage to eternal life. He stood in our place, He filled the gap and all of a sudden that emptiness, the separation that we've been talking about was filled.

To understand the hope, the future, the eternity that we have in God's Son, Jesus, means we first have to understand about our sin and separation from God. Now that we have done that, make sure you continue to the next chapter to learn more about Jesus and what it means to follow Him.

Questions

- What do you think happens when you die?

- Do you believe in heaven and hell? Why or why not?

- Can you think of things you have done that have separated you from God?

- Why do you think God wants to save you from eternal death?

- What are you prepared to do, to no longer be separated from God?

4. Jesus

4. Jesus

Jesus – no matter what you think of Him, He is man who has shaped our history and is shaping our future.

He was born a Jew in Bethlehem, Israel. To tell you the date of His birth is simple – because in most parts of the world, our calendar still counts back to that day. Don't you think it is strange that regardless of religion, country or culture we all use Jesus as the reference point of time?

He lived most of His life in a place called Galilee.
He was a carpenter.
He was a teacher.
He was a prophet.
There are historical writings that say He performed miracles.

If that's all there was to say about Jesus – then perhaps His life wouldn't have been that important – but there is so much more to Him than that.

The ultimate sacrifice starts and ends with Jesus.

In the last chapter we learnt that sin is the separation from God and the price of that is death. Every time we fall short of the perfection God intended for us we sin – on our own there is no way out - but because God loves us so much, He realised that the only way to save us from this was to pay the price Himself. He did this with the ultimate sacrifice – which starts and ends with Jesus.

Jesus was the Son of God. Before He came to earth there were many prophecies given about a man referred to as the Messiah – the anointed one chosen by God to redeem His people.

He lived on earth as an example to us – a life without sin.

He was the Son of God living on earth – fully man, fully God.
The authorities and spiritual leaders at the time didn't like what Jesus was claiming and eventually they worked together to have Him murdered in one of the most gruesome, public deaths - a crucifixion.

It was at that point that Jesus performed His greatest miracle. Three days after being killed two women went to His tomb to find it empty and soon after many people found Jesus alive again.

He faced the powers of death and overcame them to bring life.

The price He paid, the fulfilment of prophetic writings, the overcoming of death and the evil forces in our world were all done that we may no longer have eternal separation from God but an eternal relationship, eternal life.

At one point Jesus said: "I am the resurrection and the life. Anyone who believes in me will live, even after dying. Everyone who lives in me and believes in me will never die." (John 11:25-26)

One of the writers of the Bible (Paul in Romans 10:10) told us, that if you want to make a decision to follow Jesus then you need to believe in your heart that He is the Son of God and was raised from the dead and openly declare that Jesus is Lord of your life. If you want to do this then I'd suggest you find someone you can openly declare this with and pray this prayer with them:

> *Dear God – I thank you that you created me with a purpose. I know that I do things wrong that separate me from how you intended our relationship to be but I thank You that you sent your Son Jesus to die and overcome death to save me from my sin, and give me eternal life. Today I make the choice to follow you. In Jesus name – Amen.*

If you prayed that prayer, then make sure you find someone you can talk to. If there isn't anyone you know you can do this with then please contact us on the contact page at www.bethechurch.org.au.

Questions

- Who do you think Jesus was?

- Do you believe He was the Son of God?

- Why do you think He was murdered the way He was?

- What do you think of the life He lived?

- Do you believe He is still alive today?

- Are you prepared to follow Jesus with your life?

5. The Holy Spirit

5. The Holy Spirit

Just before Jesus left this world he said "wait for the gift my Father promised – the Holy Spirit" (Acts 1:4).

So what or who is the Holy Spirit?

The Holy Spirit has all the characteristics of God and plays a huge part in our life as we learn to be a follower of Jesus.

There is a point in our relationship with God where we are filled with the Holy Spirit. The Bible says He lives inside of us (1 Corinthians 3:16), He guides us into truth (John 16:13), He is our counsellor and teacher (John 14:26), He leads us (Romans 8:14), and is there for us in times of weakness and prayer (Romans 8:26). Part of relationship with God is learning to hear the Holy Spirit and respond to what He is saying to us.

When John was writing to some of the early churches he said (1 John 2:6) that if we want to be a follower of Jesus we need to live like Jesus lived. Jesus also said (John 14:12) that if we follow His life, we will be able to do even greater things than He has done.

The Holy Spirit gives us power to live as Jesus lived.

When you stop and think about that, it's almost impossible to comprehend. Jesus raised people from the dead, healed thousands of people, cast out demons, walked on water, fed thousands of people from a few loaves of bread and some fish, turned water into wine, loved people who were outcasts of society and so much more.

But its because of the Holy Spirit that we can do all the things that Jesus did and more. Jesus said that we will receive power when the Holy Spirit comes upon us (Acts 1:8). That's the same power that Jesus had – a super natural power that allows us to live like Jesus in this world. We have to remember that the purpose of this is to point people towards God – to go into the world as His witnesses. In some ways, if we call ourselves a follower of Jesus and don't live a life that reflects His power, then what kind of witness are we being?

Questions

- Describe what you think the Holy Spirit is?

- Do you think the Holy Spirit is active in our world today? Why or why not?

- Why do you think Jesus described the Holy Spirit as a gift?

- What are the parts of Jesus' life that you want your life to look more like?

6. The Church

6. The Church

When Jesus left the earth His followers began meeting together every day, sharing meals and showing others what it meant to follow Jesus (Acts 2:42-47). This was the first church and in some ways, church should be no different today.

The church is not a building, but a community of people who are gathering together for a common cause.

One way of describing the church is all the people who have ever lived in the world at any time that have believed in Jesus – that's like the global church.

The other way to describe the church is the local gathering of people who are exploring what it means to be a follower of Jesus. This is a place where you can belong. A place where people are following Jesus' teaching – learning to love God and learning to love other people.

The church is not a building but a community of people.

Now that you have read the other chapters on Christian Stuff, while we hope it has answered some of your questions, we also hope you have a lot more questions that you want answered. Things like:

What does it mean to be baptised?
What is communion?
How can I help others like Jesus did?
Why do people sing songs in church?
What are my spiritual gifts?
Why does the church ask for money and what does it use it for?
How do I tell other people about Jesus?

Part of us following Jesus is about changing the way we live – so asking questions is okay. He says that if we are prepared to give up our life to follow Him – we will gain our best life, which He wants us to live to its fullest (John 10:10).

God has gifted you and put a dream inside of you. He loves you and has a purpose for your life that fits into the plan He has for His kingdom. Paul described it this way... The church is a body – we each have a part to play, but each part of the body has a different role (1 Corinthians 12:12-31).

Sometimes people might let you down, hurt or offend you, but working through these things is part of learning to love one another. The writer of Hebrews says that we should never give up meeting together (Hebrews 10:25).

Being part of a community of people, a church, will help you to keep finding answers to your questions and find your place in the body that God wants you to play.

If you haven't found a church yet, let us know and we can help you find a church near you.

Questions

- What do you think of church?

- What has been your previous experience with church?

- Do you believe that God intended the journey of life to be done with other people? Why or why not?

- How do you believe God has gifted you?

- What do you think your purpose in life is?

- Would you like to be part of a church?

- What other questions do you have about being a follower of Jesus?

What's Next?

What's Next?

It's likely that having read this book, some of your questions have been answered, but it is more likely that you have many more questions. That's part of what it means to be a Christian. We are on a life long journey to understand and build a relationship with Jesus.

To continue exploring what all this Christian stuff is all about I'd suggest starting to do three things regularly in your life:

1. Read your Bible

Make sure you get yourself a copy of the Bible and find a way each day to read it. You could start with the passages referenced in this book. This is the word of God and becomes the foundation for you to build your own relationship with Jesus. By reading everyday you can learn more about who He is, His character, His plan for humanity, His plan for your life and by looking at the example of how Jesus lived you can find ways to apply much of the Bible in your own life today.

2. Pray

Find a time each day to pray. This is another important part of how you can build your own relationship with Jesus. Prayer just begins by speaking to God in your own words. Tell Him what you want to thank Him for, spend some time reflecting on the things you may have done wrong and asking Him for forgiveness and finish by asking for the help you need in your life or the lives of those you are connected to.

3. Gather with a church community

One of the most important things to do is find a church community that you can become a part of. It is here that you can learn from others, they can learn from you and together find ways to tell others what this Christian Stuff is all about.

If you have any questions, need help with a Bible reading plan, learning how to pray or finding a church community, then you can get in touch with us via the contact form at:
www.bethechurch.org.au

www.ingramcontent.com/pod-product-compliance
Lightning Source LLC
Chambersburg PA
CBHW042120040426
42449CB00003B/126